copyright © 2019 by LaVerne Jackson-Harvey Ph.D.

All Rights Reserved. No part of this book may be reproduced or transmitted in any form or by any means, electronic or mechanical, including photocopying, recording, or by any information storage and retrieval system, without written permission from the author. For information please email Rashida@Ella-York.com

LaVerne Jackson-Harvey, Ph.D. Publishing

Charlotte, NC

Visit our website at

www.LaverneJHarvey.com

First e-book Edition: November 2019

First Text Edition: November 2019

ISBN-10:
ISBN-13:
978-0-9909119-4-4

Table of Contents

PREFACE	5
PAIN	7
COUNT YOUR BLESSINGS	8
FORGIVENESS	10
A MOTHER'S TOUCH	12
DON'T GIVE UP	14
FACE YOUR FEARS	16
SEE THE BEAUTY IN ME	17
THROUGH THE EYES OF BABIES	18
RISE	19
BELIEVE IN YOURSELF	20
LIFE'S JOURNEY	22
DREAM THE POSSIBLE	24
SMILE	25
SELF-DOUBT CAN HURT	26
WE ARE SISTERS	28
CELEBRATION OF LIFE	30
THE BOWL OF LIFE	31
IT'S ALL ABOUT THE CHILDREN	32
NOT GOOD ENOUGH	34
WHY ME? WHY NOT ME?	35

DO NOT LET LIFE CIRCUMSTANCES LIMIT YOUR OUTCOME	36
KEEP ON KEEPING ON	38
KEEP THE FAITH	39
PAY IT FORWARD	40
YOU ARE NOT ALONE	41
THE BOX	42
THE MASK	43
SILENCE	44
STRIVE FOR EXCELLENCE	45
FIND YOUR STRENGTH	46
A RAY OF HOPE	47
SADNESS - A TUNNEL TO THE SOUL	48
CALM	49
ANGER	50
SMALL SACRIFICES	51
IN HER SHOES	52
A SEASON OF HOPE	54
SOLITUDE	56
DON'T SWAY	57
LOVE	58
IT'S SO HARD TO SAY GOODBYE (FATHER)	60
THE GRADUATE	62
HOME FOR THE HOLIDAYS	63

EMBRACE YOUR NEXT ADVENTURE	64
A LETTER TO MY FATHER	66
BREEZE	68
THE SAXOPHONE	69
TOXIC PEOPLE	70
FIND YOUR WINGS	71
YOUR ENDLESS LOVE	72
I LOVE ME	74
BLACK GIRLS MANTRA OR AFFIRMATION	74
DAYDREAMING	76
CONTROL YOUR DESTINY	77
TIME – MAKE EVERY SECOND COUNT	78
INSPIRATIONAL THOUGHTS AND QUOTES	79
ABOUT THE AUTHOR	82
CONTACT THE AUTHOR	84

Preface

Poetry for the Soul is written from the heart. It addresses the stories of life each of us must face. As a poet, I write poetry that addresses life circumstances which are not only unique to me, but to others. It comes from my soul when I write about forgiveness, love, hope, loss of love ones, pain, loving who you are, family, and not giving up when you are challenged by your story.

It was an inspiration to me when a dear friend told me that my poetry was "Picasso with words". That stayed with me because I sometimes would believe my words were meant only for me. But, when I shared them with others, they related to my story and said they needed the message I wrote.

In writing many of my poems, I believe a message was being sent to me. I was being counseled by a higher being who was sending me words I needed to hear. I feel it is my responsibility to share them with others. There were times in my life when I did not believe in myself and this beautiful poem, "Believe in Yourself" came to me in full text. I said to myself that GOD was sending me a message.

I started writing poetry at the young age of fifty. I didn't consider myself creative, but my gift shined at that stage in my life. Poetry is very personal and when you share it, you are sharing your soul and deeply rooted emotions that are private to you. I open my heart to you and hope these words will touch you in some way and help you become stronger and inspired in your story.

I would like to thank all of you who have been a part of my life's story. I thank you for your encouragement, support, and love in my life's journey. Enjoy *Poetry for the Soul and Poems from the Heart*.

Pain

Pain
Sharp
Deep
To the core
Bottled up but cannot open
Deeper inside and out
The emotion is closed
It's hard to expose
Turning, churning, oozing as it implodes
Out with a sigh
Hurtful no lie
Ease, relief, slowly opening up from inside
Pain no more

Count Your Blessings

We all have blessings that are a part of our lives
The ability to wake up and see another day
The ability to see the beauty of God's work
To hear sounds of our environment and nature
To speak words of encouragement and communicate with others
The joy of being with our family and friends
Food to nourish our bodies and share with our loved ones

A lifetime partner to share our love
A roof over our heads for shelter and comfort
The opportunity to give back to our community
The thrill of meeting a goal we've set for ourselves
The ability to see the light during our darkest hour and
Hope for a better day and peace around the world

The willingness to choose hope over hate during tumultuous times in our country
The ability to dream the possible
The capacity to love unconditionally
The aptitude to learn
The fortitude to provide guidance, values, and support for our children
The optimism to believe in the possibilities and not be afraid of challenges
The strength to not let fear rule our actions and stop us from living
But face our fears
With zest and zeal for life

This time of year touches our hearts in so many ways
It allows us to enjoy the moment and reflect on the past
It allows us to smile as we think of our loved ones no longer with us
We have so much in which to be thankful
Life, love, happiness, health, friends, family, accomplishments, compassion for others, and God in our lives

Share your gifts to impact on the life of someone in need of hope
Who may be in pain, feel hopeless, alone, alienated, and not worthy
Use your compassion to make a difference in the lives of others
Keep your faith, embrace, and share your bounty
Be thankful for your life's circumstances and
Count your blessings

Forgiveness

We live in a time where there is an abundance of pain,
hurt, uncertainty, and social ills
This can sometimes bring out the worst in our character
Blinding us in seeing the good that surrounds us
We focus on the negative
This affects us and people who have offended us, be it
family, friends, or foe
It can lead to anger, fear, and unforgiveness

Forgiveness can help you release some of this ill will
When you don't forgive others
You give them power over your emotions
It takes so much energy to internalize hatred and
resentment
It can fester and burn out the light of joy and happiness
Unforgiveness can spread like a cancer that invades the
innocence of our soul
It can make us capable of actions we never envisioned
ourselves capable of committing
It is a mood breaker that takes away the love we have for
others and ourselves

We must learn to release the anger, hate,
and negative will
This will allow us to mend our inner spirit
Leading to serenity, joy, goodwill, and tranquility
We must forgive ourselves for not being perfect and
mistakes we have made
And pain we may have inflicted on others in our past
Forgiveness is a powerful aphrodisiac

We were taught the power of forgiveness
through our God
He showed us through example
The power of inner faith, love, and hope
And how to forgive our enemies
Do not let dislike for another person impede your joy
and growth
Let go and let GOD
Live your life in harmony

A Mother's Touch

As a child, we are taught many things
How to tie our shoes?
How to use the bathroom?
How to properly wash our hands?
How to put on our clothes?
How to eat a healthy meal?
How to speak?

This is taught with unconditional love
by our mothers
Mothers have the touch to make the sore hurt less
Make food taste better
Make the long road trip seem shorter
Mothers sometime have eyes
in the back of their head
They see your mischief
And you wonder, how in the world did they know?
They discipline you
While loving you none the less

Mothers request that you get involved in activities
That will help you grow
They do this sometimes without your say
And you want to say no way
As time goes by and you excel in your activities
You say thank you for being the adult
Thank you for saying yes when I said no
And thank you for saying no when I wanted you to
say yes

They run from one event to the next tired
And patiently waiting for you to finish
With a smile on their faces and internally exhausted
They take you to your next event
A mother's love is irreplaceable
A mother's touch is forever
It is gentle, loving, guiding, and firm
All at once
Making you into the wonderful adult you are

Don't Give Up

When you feel all hope is gone
Don't give Up
When you feel no one hears you
Don't give up
When you no longer see your purpose
Don't give up
When your love ones have transitioned to the great beyond
Don't give up
When you feel alienated, not appreciated, and invisible
Don't give up
When sadness consumes your heart and soul
Don't give up
When you allow negative self-talk to consume your internal and external conversations
Don't give up

When you feel your plate is full and is about to tip over
Don't give up
When the pain seems relentless
Don't give up
When you feel you can't take back bad decisions
Don't give up
When others don't acknowledge or value your accomplishments
Don't give up

When you hear you can't be successful and not
what you can achieve
Don't give up
When you are judged by the color of your skin and
not your intellect and gifts
Don't give up

When someone takes advantage of your gender and
feel they have a right to your body and your mind
Don't give up
When you have special needs and abilities
Don't give up
When you ask why me when the question should be
why not me?
Don't give up

When you are discriminated against because of your
race, culture, language, age, sex, and religion
Don't give up
When racism raises its ugly head
Don't give up
Don't give up
You are stronger than you think
You have a purpose
You can face life's ugly circumstances, naysayers,
and haters
And stand on top and reach your goals
You are the captain of your ship
Through God all things are possible
You must keep on keeping on
And know you have control of your destiny
Don't give up

Face Your Fears

An emotion that stops you in your tracks
Causing you to feel tense
Paralyzing
Heart beat fast
Pulse increasing
Anxiety high
Makes you afraid to take risks
Sometimes stifling your growth
For fear of failure or consequences
You avoid the unknown
Staying in the dark
Afraid of the outcome
Sometimes you live with the unknown
For fear of the known

Fear can challenge your desire to live
Frightening you to the point you don't want to go anywhere
It can lead to phobias

As difficult as it is to face your demons
You must not let it stop you from living
Take the steps to face your fears
Live your life to the fullest
Challenging yourself to move, not freeze, in time
Take steps to live your life
Face your fears

See The Beauty In Me

Many times we see our flaws
More vividly than anyone else
My stomach is flabby and not so tight
My thighs are thick and not quite right
My bottom jiggles just a little bit
And sometimes is flat when I sit
My muscles in my arms have disappeared
And my breast has decided to take a rest
My eyes are small and big and bright
My hair is black, blonde, red-oh what a sight
I can't go out, no not tonight
I am too tall and can't find a date
I am too short and why is my date late
I see myself in the mirror
My reflection looks at me
And you know what
I like what I see
I see the beauty in me

Through The Eyes Of Babies

God's gift to parents
To love, guide, and mold into productive citizens
Babies are innocent
Not aware of the world around them
Open to new ideas
They see people as one
Do not discriminate
Because of the color of your skin, race, creed,
national origin, and religion
They are like sponges
Soaking up knowledge
Eager to learn
They need unconditional love
Their eyes sparkle with the excitement
Of their next adventure
They bring joy, love and hope
Babies fill voids in our heart
As adults we need to view life
Through the eyes of babies
Seeing their innocence
Eagerness to learn
And imparting love to those in their presence

Rise

down
falling further in
trying to stand
weighted by demons
holding you still
not moving
slowly you make progress
floating to the top
rising above pain, hurt, bad judgement and demons
seeing the light

Believe In Yourself

Believe in yourself
You are worthy
You are capable
Believe in who you are and where you want to go
And know you will reach your goals
Do not let others define you
Limit your potential and
Break your spirit
Life is full of ups and downs
Highs and lows
It's up to you how you handle these difficult times
in your life
You can let self-doubt rule
And stay down, waddling in sorry
Or
You can let hope lift you high
Push you beyond belief and
Closer to your dreams
Knowing the process requires you to
Crawl, walk, and then run
With your head held high
A stride in your walk and
Confidence in who you are

Believe in yourself
Even when others don't
When you are told you can't reach your goal
Use this as a challenge to propel yourself into action
Because action speaks louder then words

Believe in yourself
Love yourself
Challenge yourself
The more you believe in yourself
The more you will achieve
Knowing that life is full of challenges, fears, and inhibitions,
Embrace your potential
Embrace your gifts and
Believe that you will SUCCEED

Life's Journey

Sometimes events in our life take us for a loop
The element of surprise and disbelief
The fear of the unknown
The challenges that's ahead of us are insurmountable

We live our life
Our love, our family value and strengths, our accomplishments
Our children, weddings, deaths, and events of life

As we reflect on our journey
We must know that every event in our life will make us stronger
You may not see that as it happens

Through our trials and tribulations
We must dig deep into our soul
For strength, hope, and faith in God

As we face this bump in the road
We must remember that life itself is a bump in the road
It slows us down so we can maneuver around the obstacles
And figure out a way to get over it and
Find our way to our destinations

We sometimes do not want to talk
Negative self-talk finds its way into our mind
We feel we are alone
And no one cares or understands
And we ask why me?

This is a natural response to some
When we face life's challenges
After the shock though we need to move on
And face it head-on

We must remember the love of our children
Our family, our friends, our church, our pastor, and our GOD
They are there for you and know you are not alone on this journey

Where there is hurt and pain
There is also hope and courage and
The knowledge that we don't give up
But will fight to the end
With all our being
We have so much to live for
And many more life challenges to face and overcome

Dream The Possible

To dream the possible
You must believe
You must dream it
To receive it

Many of us do not dream
Because we believe the impossible
We are told we cannot achieve it
We are not encouraged to dream
Beyond our realities

Some of our realities limit our dreams
We do not have food in abundance
A roof over our heads may be mobile, there are no guarantees
Education provides us possibilities
But opportunities are not always equal

We must encourage our children
No matter their life circumstances
They must not limit their goals
But be bold beyond their imagination
Because they deserve the best

They are worthy regardless
Poverty should not limit their dreams
Naysayer's should not limit their dreams
They need to be exposed to the possibilities
And encouraged to dream the possible

Smile

When life sends you a lemon
It's hard to find joy
Hard to remember the happiness that brings you
purpose and peace
Frowns become a part of your daily expressions
You see the negative
And positive thoughts evade you
There is hope
During this time, you must turn that frown around
Find what makes you happy
Love those that are dear to you
And pray for serenity
You must turn that frown upside down
And reclaim your joy and smile
A smile can touch the hearts of others
And let them know you see them
You appreciate them
And show love
It can melt your heart
And help alleviate the pain
Find your happiness, and simply smile

Self-Doubt Can Hurt

Self-doubt can hurt
It can deter you from reaching your goals
It can limit your outcome
Causing you not to believe in yourself

Many times it can be negative self-talk
Making you question why you should be blessed
You don't deserve this break
No one will support your efforts
It's not good enough

Self-doubt can hurt
It can keep you down
Discouraging you to believe
And put out the effort
Needed to succeed

Many times it's ingrained deep
In your being
Causing you to be your own worst enemy
To see the worst verses the best
In what you've accomplished

Self-doubt can be changed to confidence
Change negative self-talk
To positive self-talk
Believe you are worthy
And accept your blessing
When given a compliment

For touching someone's heart
Say thank you
Know God gave you this gift
To help others see the light, to believe

Self-doubt can hurt
Both self confidence and believing in yourself
Can take the hurt away
And help you to grow
Positively everyday

We Are Sisters

We are sisters
Linked together by the bond of our mother
The blood that streams through our veins
The father that sacrificed for us
Who was gone too soon

We are sisters
Who shared our life circumstances
Some good and some bad
But knowing we are always
There for each other

We are sisters
That rejoiced in the birth of our children
Who supported each other
In struggles

We are sisters
Who shared makeup and clothes
Did each other's hair
Shared recipes
Had fights and made up

We are sisters
Who know pain, joy, peace, happiness, togetherness
Challenges, hurt, love, struggles, motherhood
Through it all
The main staple is that
We depend on each other

We are strong women
We have experienced events in our lives
That we made it through because we had each other
We gave each other strength and
We were good listeners

One thing we can depend on
Is our love for each other
Even when we go through trying times
Our bond is unbreakable

God gave us to each other
A gift from above
We can survive all things through Christ
Because of that love
We are sisters to the end!

Celebration of Life

This is the time of year for celebration
We celebrate the lives of our love ones who are no longer with us
We celebrate with our families and friends the joy of the season
We celebrate our life so that we may enrich some else's life

We celebrate the birth of Jesus Christ
May we bestow our blessings to those who are experiencing trials and tribulations, grief, and hard times to keep the faith
And commemorate this season of hope

This is the season for joy, happiness, peace, love, and giving
May you embrace this holiday season with zest and a celebration of life

The Bowl Of Life

The bowl of doubt
dull
not shining
not polished
not worthy
not of value
cheap
full of air
not of substance
empty
insignificant
not good enough
The bowl of life
fill it to the rim with
joy
peace
hope
knowledge
love
strength
belief
faith
will power
family
full of substance
values
priceless gems of life

It's All About The Children

We must not forget that we were once children
Bright eyes, inquisitive, talkative, hyperactive, and
questioning everything
We had dreams and aspirations
We played bear, hopscotch, red light, marbles, mud
bakery, caught junebugs, and fireflies
Our imagination was endless
We were allowed to be kids
Not trying to be adults before our time

We are now adults who have had these experiences
that make us who we are today
It's all about the children
Kids today have so many strikes against them
Many grow up way before their time
They want to be adults and are exposed to adult
situations
Many skipped being a child because of their
realities

It is all about the children
Who are not allowed to use their imagination
Many have no guidance
And behave in deplorable ways
They don't value your life or their own
Many are misdirected and have questionable values

We must save our children
We must believe in our children
Allowing them the opportunity to
Grow into productive and loving adults
We must all do our part to save our children
Because when it's all said and done
It's all about the children
Our future

Not Good Enough

Try Hard
Work 110%
Do your best
But
You are not good enough

Believe in yourself
Set high goals
I will decide your future
Because
You are not good enough

Get a good education
Work harder and smarter
However you don't fit in
Because
You're not good enough

Do not let others
Break you down
Devaluing your hard work
Silencing your voice
Standing in judgment of your best effort
Think smart
Work hard
Believe in yourself
And know
You Are Good Enough!

Why Me? Why Not Me?

Why Me?
Why not me!
For God determines what's right you see
I must keep the faith
When I'm feeling down
And find a way to turn it around
Why me? Why not me!
We often ask
Because God has given us a given path
Which way will you stroll
When your time will come
Only God knows what the outcome will be
But you have the power
To choose eternity

Do Not Let Life Circumstances Limit Your Outcome

Some people are blessed with material riches, opportunities for success are a part of life's expectations. They are privileged to have their basic needs met...employment, health care, education, food, and housing.

They go to the best schools, take the most rigorous college preparation classes, they are taught by highly qualified teachers who have high expectations for them and they attend summer camps or precollege programs. Their future is set and it's up to them to take what is given to them and make their future better.

Others are products of poverty, food is not promised, a roof over their heads is not guaranteed, unemployment, single family household, living paycheck to paycheck. Disappointments and failures are a part of life. No medical services are available, and violence is a part of their daily being.

Their children attend schools where some teachers don't believe in them, they have low expectations for the children. Many are not highly qualified, and work for a paycheck-not the dividend of making a positive difference in the life of a child.

Children are told to take high school classes that will not prepare them for college but for minimum wage jobs, and they do not attend summer camps and Precollege programs…the streets are their summer opportunities.

In spite of these circumstances, these children have what it takes to be successful. History has shown that many students who are products of families with less means have triumphed and been successful in spite of life's negative curve and many with the means and the foundation have failed in spite of having the best of everything.

We must teach all our children that in spite of life circumstances, positive outcomes are available to them.

Keep On Keeping On

When life throws you a curve ball
Keep on keeping on
When it seems like you've reached rock bottom
Keep on keeping on
If you hear negative self talk
Deep in your subconscious
Turn the negative to a positive and
Keep on keeping on
Don't let the doubting Thomases
Plot your destiny
Plan your path
Walk the walk and
Talk the talk
And keep on keeping on

Keep The Faith

Sometimes in life we make choices
That have negative consequences
The punishment can sometimes seem harsh
But in spite of it all, life goes on
The circumstances you are experiencing are not ideal
But you have to make the most of your situation
Take this time to reflect on
What you have done
What you have learned and
Where you plan to go from here

The thing about life experiences, good or bad is
There is always a lesson to be taught
You must learn from your decisions
If it was a good decision, you may want to do it again
If it was a bad decision, you must learn
To not repeat it and reflect on what you would do differently

Know that there are people
Who believe in you
Who love you and
Who want the best for you
Keep the faith
Keep believing in yourself
Know that life can be better for you
Everyone deserves a second chance
Make Yours Count!

LaVerne Jackson-Harvey, Ph.D.

Pay It Forward

Try a little kindness
You can accomplish a lot
Don't let negativity
Keep you in a bad spot
A "thank you, may I help you"
Is just a way to show
That common courtesy many people still know
A smile, a nod, an acknowledgement can go
Much further then you will ever imagine
It can impact on people in need of knowing that
they are not invisible
And can catapult them to succeed
Pay it forward
And share kindness

Because you don't know whose life you may change

You Are Not Alone

Sometimes when you experience loss
There is emptiness in your heart
You feel weak
You feel alone
You feel like the burden of the world is on your shoulders
Even when you are surrounded by the people you love
You still feel alone
You feel all the pain in your soul
Knowing you will not see their smile, hear their voices, and
The comforting words of your loved ones
Your joy is wavering
During this difficult time, you must maintain hope
Hold on to your faith as well as your family
And know that God is with you
And you are not alone

The Box

A box has four corners
And is enclosed at the top
It can be full of faith, hope, love, joy,
Peace, long suffering, and temperance
Or
It can be full of hate, rejection, fear,
Discrimination, prejudices, and negative myths
It can obtain tools of success
That can take you a long way
Or
It can obtain instruments of oppression
That will have a negative stay
The box can be full of knowledge
And have staying powers
The box is like a person
It can have a top and bottom
It is full of possibilities
What will you put in your box?

The Mask

The face shows
What you want to see
But is that person
Really me
The smile, the look, the joy, the sound
Deep down inside it's really a frown
You see what you want to see
The mask shows a part of me
Look deeper and you will see
Who's really inside
The real me

Silence

A voice with no sound
Speaking but not heard
Screaming and shouting
Wanting to release
No one's listening to the cry
Life continues to move on
Existing in a bowl
Slowly your voice is heard
Silence turns to sound

Strive For Excellence

Strive for Excellence
Challenge yourself to go the extra mile
And not settle for less
But to always do your very best
Life is full of roadblocks
Confront each hurdle
And use it as a challenge to reach higher
When you are faced with difficulties
Know that is part of life
You must figure out a way to get around the problem
To move beyond the dilemma
And advance to the next level
Knowing you will have barriers
Life is an obstacle course
It has many twists and turns
It's how you play the game
That will make a difference
Work hard, don't quit
Embrace challenges and
Disappointments
Know you are strong and have inner strength
Believe and
Strive for excellence

Find Your Strength

Your heart is broken
Due to the loss of a loved one
You feel broken
With the thoughts of tomorrow that will never come. The smiles that will not exist other than in your memories. The sound of your voice that will never be heard again

Strength comes from within
It's hard to accept this when you feel weak and confused and others depend on you for guidance. Events or thoughts that normally would not affect you become intensified during this moment of sadness.

During this time, you can count each memory as a blessing.
You move beyond existing but learn to live again
Embracing your family, friends, and your faith.
You find your inner strength and know you don't have to be strong all the time because you are human and your emotions run deep.
God will give you no more than you can bear.
Seek his guidance and love yourself
And find your strength.

A Ray Of Hope

Let not life's circumstances dim your light
Of
What could and can be
Believe
That you deserve all that's offered if you put out equal effort
Continue to believe in your potential
Never question your capability
Strive for excellence
Believe in yourself
Believe in your future
Believe in who you want to be
Do not let others dim your light
Let it shine bright
Because
There is always that ray of hope

Sadness – A Tunnel To The Soul

A hole that was full of joy in our heart
A seeping of life, energy, love that will no longer be
A moment in time that everyone will see

Sadness digs deep in our core
When our loved one's we will see no more
Spirits low, energy depleted, pain interceding where
joy once was abound
Knowing that this person is nowhere around

Life goes on as hard as it is
The love that was shared will always be there

Feeling the moments of sadness
And grateful for the moments of gladness
That will always fill that hole
A tunnel to our soul

Calm

A sense of peace

Solitary thoughts that cause

A release of emotions

Leading to openness, clarity, and a sigh of relief

Removing stress

Overcoming the storms

That affect your being

Leading to calm

Anger

A harsh reaction to a situation
Brings out mixed emotions
Causing you not to have clear focus
But to release pent-up emotions and frustrations
Many times causing you not to make rational decisions
It can cause tremendous harm
You react and then you think

You are upset because of how circumstances affect you
Anger can bring out the worst in you
When not channeled to positive solution
Lack of control
Sometimes you are on a roll
Causing you to explode
Leading to violent resolution

Anger can be harsh, relentless, volatile, hurtful, and painful
When not addressed and resolved
Anger is an emotion that can be channeled
To not harm yourself and others through mental or physical abuse

Release those emotions to make better decisions
Strengthen yourself and redirect your rage to make choices
That will guide your future not the moment

Small Sacrifices

Sacrifices in life is paramount
Although we may not know why or how
Life is full of sacrifices
That may be big or small
No matter, the results are the same
They are for the best
They build character
We must make choices
Always wondering if they were the right decisions
In light of the outcome
The decision for some
Is easy to make
Out of sacrifices come results
That can bring joy for a lifetime

In Her Shoes

Walking in the shoes of phenomenal women
All styles, shapes, size, color, culture, religion
Unique to each woman
They are the foundation to our frame
Carrying all the load we have too bare

As women, we have characteristics
That are as unique as we are
We are loving mothers, wives, sisters, aunties and friends
We love our children and spouses unconditionally
We value our family
We wear many hats; chauffeur, cheerleader, doctor, friend,
Role model, caregiver, supporter, lover, comforter, teacher, educator, mother, believer, and
provider…to name a few

Life throws many challenges at us
And some are harder to overcome than others
But through our faith, determination, creativity,
And resiliency, we survive
When we look at life and our stories, we wear them well

Shoes comes in all styles, shapes, cost, color, and sizes and fits the personality of the women who wear them. They accentuate the beauty of the woman.

Providing them with the support to move forward in life
And striding with their head held high
And confidence to take on a goal

The beauty of women shines through from the inside and out
And their stories are unique to their life circumstances
Struggles, successes, families, obstacles, and socio-economic status

In your shoes you should love who you are
See the beauty in you and
Acknowledge your strengths to overcome challenges and become the beautiful woman you are

A Season Of Hope

A Season of Hope
Allows us to grow, believe
And know through sheer determination
You can experience and survive the changes of life
Hope allows us to see
The future where possibilities exist
It helps us to forget the
Pain of the past and know life can improve
Hope allows us to heal
And see the joy
Hope helps us to believe in ourselves and others
It lets us know that through
Trials and tribulations there is light at the end of the
tunnel
Hope allows us to see the best in ourselves
And forgive mistakes we've made in the past
It helps us to get up in the morning
And face a new day
Hope lifts us up when we fall
Not allowing us to stay down
But to stand tall
Hope challenges us to think
Beyond the moment
And see the future
Hope allows us to see
During our darkest hours
That this to shall pass
Hope will lift you high and
Not allow you to fall into the abyss

A ray of hope shines bright and is electrifying,
Shocking us to new heights and will not allow us to
fall into harms way
But through God see a better way
A Season of Hope
Is ongoing
Allowing you to change with life circumstances
Lifts your spirits when you are down and
Keeps you believing through your faith

Solitude

A time for reflection
Finding and hearing your inner voice
You can go deep within your soul
Reliving your life story
All that makes you who you are
Your love, family, friends, and faith
That are weaved into your tapestry
Your thoughts are deep
In the sound of silence
Solitude provides peace

Don't Sway

Don't sway
You've come too far
To not make your way
Difficult as it is to stay focus
You must stay on track
If you've gotten off
Then it's time to get back

The future is yours
The opportunities are plenty
Don't let distractions get in the way
Because there are many

You will be celebrating
Reaching your goals with
Your family and friends
Whose been there to the end
They will be there to cheer you own
And in unison they will say
Well done
You didn't sway
You did it your way

Love

Love is a four letter word
That evokes many emotions
It has different meanings for different people
Love wakes the inner being
Touching you where few can reach
Love can be passionate
When shared with a significant person in your life
Your soul mate
Love can be unconditional
Such as love between a parent and child
Love knows no boundaries
And is experienced across the world in all cultures
The art of love may be expressed differently
But the meaning is the same
Love can lift you up
When you are feeling down
It can bring joy that is unimaginable
Love can cause pain
When others abuse your emotions
Causing you to shutdown
Love can also open up feelings
And enjoyment you didn't know exist
Love can be everlasting
Or it can be cut short
Love will allow you to open up to others
And not have to wear the mask
Second-guessing if the feelings are mutual
Love can heal a nation
Love is powerful

LaVerne Jackson-Harvey, Ph.D.

It comes in many layers
Not exposed at once
Love is universal
It can be shared between family, friends, and special people you meet
Love can also cause you to not
Always make sound judgments
When you follow your heart
This amazing feeling may not come easy to some
Because of their life circumstances
And their emptiness of not feeling needed
Not receiving unconditional love
Or being a part of someone else's life
Open your heart
Share your gift with others
And enjoy the feelings of love

It's So Hard To Say Goodbye (Father)

As life takes us through many trials and tribulations
The loss of a parent is one of the hardest
experiences we as children will go through
A parent provides guidance, unconditional love, and
values to make us who we are
Our parents believe in us when we don't believe in
ourselves
They show their love when sometimes
It is hard to say I Love You
The loss of a love one
Can cause pain that is deep
Sharp
And to the core of our being

Your father may be gone
But he will not be forgotten
Cherish the many years you were
Blessed to share with him
Knowing that he will always be
In your heart, your memories, and your core
Always know that God will not give you more than
you can bear
Especially when we must say goodbye

May God continue during this time of loss bless you
and your family
Take each day one day at a time
And be comforted in knowing that there are people
out there who love you and

Will be there for you
During the moments of sadness
Be grateful for the moments of gladness
That will always fill that hole
A tunnel to the soul

The Graduate

Life is a journey
That has many twist and curves
Many times the road is rough
But we continue to travel our course
Because life can be bumpy
There are many turns
That led in different directions
You have to ponder which way to go
As a graduate you have traveled the right road
You have made choices that
Led to positive outcomes
You made it through high school, test, relationships
Roommates, peer pressure, trials and tribulations,
and life decisions
And now you've reached this journey in your life-
GRADUATION
This has been a goal that was long term
But now the time is near
May you continue to make choices that will
Elevate you to new heights
Challenge you intellectually
And
Take you to your next adventure
May your future continue to be bright
We salute you-Our Graduate

Home For The Holidays

The holidays bring the family together
Our hearts are open with joy
We gather to fellowship
Reflect on what we have experienced
Laughing, talking, hugging, kissing, and relishing each other's company
The food is so great
It is so plentiful
The ham, turkey, chitterlings, mac and cheese, pies, cakes, etc.
I can't get enough on my plate

The children that were small
Are now grown up and all
It is great to hear Christmas music
Rejoicing in the birth of Jesus Christ
And remembering those that are not with us
And let's not forget the gifts

Many times, when I'm asked
What do I want for Christmas?
I gladly say my health, my family,
And peace for all
While the gift giving is great
Let's remember the real meaning of Christmas

Home for Christmas
Is a wish many faraway desire
The joy is knowing you can celebrate
Wherever you are because
Home is in the heart

Embrace Your Next Adventure

Life is so funny
As a child you are taught many things
One is to prepare for your future
Not knowing what that means
Being so young you think maybe ten years ahead
Not thinking about your horizon-RETIREMENT

The road to this destination is never clear
You experience being a child and teenager and you wonder,
How did I survive this one?
Through all those experiences, good and bad
It made you stronger for what was ahead
As a teenager you dream about what you can be
How to get there, and set goals to reach your destination
The road at this point can be bumpy
But you stand your ground
Through your willpower, stubbornness, and grit
Going on to college and
Reaching one of many goals-graduation

Now that your ten years have passed you have to think ahead
Again, for the next ten years
Love may come your way and you are smitten with this
Tall, dark, and handsome man of substance who becomes your husband
This takes you on a new adventure
You are establishing your career, sharing your life with your loved one

What more can there be, you ask?
Let's see: community service, volunteering, church, and family

You are now at the point in your life where ten years add up to a new adventure—RETIREMENT
No one knows what the future holds, but you have walked a stellar past
Take this time to breathe, dream, and relax
Then run to your next adventure
Because this is not the end but a new beginning….

A Letter to My Father

Dad, I dream about who you were
How you and mom met
The void in my life
You and mom brought eleven beautiful children
Into the world
Eight boys and three girls
And I was the last child
All your children's name starts with L
The first letter of love
God took you from us at a very young age
And I was just three months old
I cannot remember your presence, your touch, your face, your smile, and
Who you were?

I know you were special because
You had a phenomenal wife
She reflected the both of you
Through her courage, strength, guidance, nurturing, and value
I know life was not easy
Providing for your family was difficult
And I'm sure we were a handful
In your pictures I see glimpses
Of you in each of us
And that makes me smile

I remember Father's Day
That was difficult for me
Everyone else did special things
To recognize their dad
But I could not relate
I remember days in school when
We drew pictures of family and
I had no image of you to draw

As I grew older there was a level of pain and regrets
Regrets for not having you to take me to school
Regrets of not having a memory of you
Regrets of not seeing your smile
Regrets of not having you to spoil me
Regrets that we could not take a family picture
Regrets that you could not come to my wedding and walk me down the aisle
Regrets that you did not meet my husband and your grandchildren
Regrets for my loss
This however did not make me less of a person

We were rich in love
I know you are a part of me
You are in my soul and being
You helped to make me who I am
You may be gone but you are not forgotten
You and mom can reignite your love in Heaven
You are my father and
I will always love you

Breeze

fresh and crisp
moving but can't be seen
you feel the touch
and see the results
but can't touch
it sends chills through you
touching you all over
never still
moving eternally
breeze

The Saxophone

I am an instrument
Smooth and crisp
I am shiny with keys
Making a joyful noise
That soothes the soul
I have a mouthpiece
That makes silence turn to sound
I am long and curvy
The breath of life
Fills my pipes
And brings amazing music
I can go high and low
And make you move
To my voice
I am a saxophone

LaVerne Jackson-Harvey, Ph.D.

Toxic People

Negative aura
A snake waiting to strike
Leaving its prey in harm's way
Not blinking, not moving
Still
Looking for a conquer
At any cost
Cannot be trusted
Only concerned for self
And to hell with others

See themselves as a gift
That others covet
Wanting to be like them

Steer yourself away from
The snake, with toxic venom
Do not allow yourself to be in striking distance
Allowing the venom to enter your system
Life is too short

Find Your Wings

Sometimes in life we feel we are falling and unable
to fly because life happens
And we feel broken

This is the time we must test our faith
Reach for hope to keep us stable
Trust God because he has a plan for us
We may not know what it is
But God will show us the way

We may struggle to hold on
Trying not to fall
Looking for balance in our life

As time goes on we become stronger
Not letting fear of failure or disappointment stop us
We look back at those experiences and lessons that
were learned

Through these trying times
We find our way and
Are now ready to soar

We find our wings and fly
To our next adventure
We know that with God's guidance
We will survive

Your Endless Love

Celebrating twenty-five years of wedding bliss
The times you've shared together is priceless.
You have experienced some good and tough times together... And the key word is together
You have been blessed.
You have shared life experiences that are dear to your heart.
The first time you met, held hands, and knew you were meant to be soul mates.
The love you shared and the day you married each other before God and your family,
Twenty- Five years ago

You embarked on a new adventure.
You became parents and imparted your wisdom and values to your children, watching them grow into wonderful adults and parents.
Seeing them get married and you becoming grandparents.
Your strength, love, and support of each other has been endless and has meant the world to you.
When a man of substance commits to a woman of character the bond is unbreakable

Twenty-five years of marriage very few people reach.
May your love bring joy and passion,
Your bond grow tighter,
Your communication remain open,
Your commitment to each other blossom, and
The gift of time be many.

May your faith help you to grow closer to each other.
Life takes us through many trials and tribulations
You've stood the test of time.
May you continue to grow together,
Through your endless love.
Reaching your next twenty-five years

I Love Me

Black Girls Mantra or Affirmation

I love myself
I love my story
I am smart
I am beautiful
I am Black girl magic
I am courageous
I am confident
I am Black girl inspired
I embrace my differences
I embrace my culture
I am descendants of African Queens
I embrace my style
I am a dreamer
I am fierce
I am strong
I am a survivor
I am special
I am blessed

I believe in myself
There is not another me
I am a unique Black girl who will become a beautiful Black woman
I see the beauty in me
I love me

Daydreaming

Daydreaming
Looking in the air
No reflection of what's there
Blank and clear
Who cares!
It provides thought
Without answers
Memories with dreams
Daydreaming take you places
That's near and dear
Provides time for introspection
A look from inside out
The stare jolts your reality

Control Your Destiny

Life can be so confusing
You are not sure which way to go
Knowing that whatever
Choice you make
Will impact your destiny
What is your destiny?
Only God knows
You are given gifts
To direct your path
The decision is yours….
To control your destiny

Time – Make Every Second Count

Moves Continuously
Without interruption
Stays still for no one
Cannot be negotiated
Cannot be paid to end
Not controlled
It epitomizes equal opportunity
Does not discriminate
Move with ease
Tick tock, tick tock, tick tock
Does not stop
We control what we do with our time
Make every second count

Inspirational Thoughts and Quotes

"Share your gifts to impact the life of someone in need of hope. Who may be in pain, feel hopeless, alone, and alienated. Use your compassion to make a difference in the lives of others."

"Unforgiveness can spread like a cancer that invades the innocence of our soul. It can make us capable of actions we never envisioned ourselves committing. It is a mood breaker that takes away the love we have for others and ourselves."

"When you don't forgive others, you give them power over your emotions"

"A mother's love is irreplaceable; a mother's touch is forever."

"As difficult as it is to face your demons, you must not let it stop you from living. Take steps to face your fear."

"When you hear you can't be successful and not what you can achieve, don't give up!"

"I see myself in the mirror, my reflection looks at me, and you know what-I like what I see. I see the beauty in me!"

"Believe in yourself!

Do not let others define you, limit your potential, and break your spirit."

"As we reflect on our journey, we must know that every event in our life will make us stronger. You may not see that as it happens."

"Where there is hurt and pain, there is hope and courage, and the knowledge that we don't give up, but we will fight to the end."

"A smile can touch the heart of others and let them know you see them."

"Why me? Why not me!"

"The box is like a person; it can have a top and bottom. It is full of possibilities. What will you put in your box?"

"Life is like an obstacle course. It has many twists and turns. It's how you play the game that will make a difference."

"Anger is an emotion that can be channeled to not harm yourself and others through mental or physical abuse."

"Out of sacrifices come results that can bring joy for a lifetime."

"The beauty of women shines through from the inside and out. Their stories are unique to their life circumstances."

"In the sound of silence solitude provides peace."

"Love is powerful and it comes in many layers. It is not exposed all at once."

"A ray of hope shines bright and is electrifying, shocking us to new heights. It will not allow us to fall into harms way, but through God see a better way."

"We must teach our children that in spite of life circumstances, positive outcomes are available to them."

About The Author

Dr. LaVerne Jackson-Harvey has over thirty years of experience in K-12 and postsecondary education in counseling, advising, research, teaching, public speaking, and program design. She began writing poetry at a late, but exciting time in her life, and has authored over 200 poems. LaVerne has published three books of poetry entitled *Life Circumstances: Don't Let Life Circumstances Limit Your Outcome, A Ray of Hope: Poems of Inspiration, and Ebony Thoughts: Poems from a Cultural Perspective*. She has also written a children's book entitled *Ruth and Her Hoots*.

LaVerne received her Bachelors degree from Claflin University, Masters degree from Bowling Green State University, and Doctorate from Marquette University.

While employed at Marquette University, LaVerne founded The Night of Black Literature, a program that allowed students and staff to read their favorite poetry by African American authors. She has recited her poetry at numerous events. LaVerne was raised in Inman, South Carolina and lived in Milwaukee, Wisconsin. She has three children and currently resides in Charlotte, North Carolina with her husband.

Contact the Author

www.LaverneJHarvey.com

Email:
Laverne.Harvey@yahoo.com

Twitter:
www.Twitter.com/LaverneJHarvey

Facebook:
www.Facebook.com/LJHPoetry

www.ingramcontent.com/pod-product-compliance
Lightning Source LLC
Chambersburg PA
CBHW030911170426
43193CB00009BA/812